Dedication

*For the children who taught me to listen,
the parents who trusted me,
and the voices that continue to grow through love, the grief, and the memories.*

I speak in more than words

Written by Tash Howlett

Copyright © 2025 - Tash Talks Communication

All rights reserved. No part of this book may be reproduced in any manner whatsoever without prior written permission of the publisher.

First Printing, 2025

Published by Tash Talks Communication
www.tashhowlett.com

Hardcover:
ISBN 978-1-7640982-9-8

Paperback:
ISBN 978-1-7643930-0-3

eBook:
ISBN 978-1-7643930-1-0

The playground's loud and laughter is strong,

the kids chat and shout all day long.

But my voice gets lost as it's small,

and wonder if you 'hear' me at all.

I want to talk and I feel it deep,
but often my words are only a peep.
The other kids chatter, laugh and sing,
words come to them like an easy thing.

But it's hard to find the words I need,
I want you to know how much I plead.
I want to share what's in my heart,
showing you me, my every part.

I feel the weight, the push, the pull,
and sometimes feel that I'm the fool.
I see you staring, brimming with hope,
longing for words, it's hard to cope.

I'm trying my best, but it may not show,
I wish you knew the lengths I go.
My mind is full and so loud in here,
my words get twisted, heavy in fear.

I'm aware of your sadness and quiet despair,
hoping I'll talk, that I'll somehow share.
But the pressure builds and rests on my chest,
will I ever pass your FUCKING test?

I feel small, feel I'm not enough,

am I seen when things are rough?

The dreams you have, I want them too,

I'm so often scared, just like you.

Then one day, I see you smile,
a cozy warmth that's kept a while.

It feels like a soft feather on my skin,
and I begin to feel, that you see me within.

In that moment, though my words are new,
I feel that now you see me too.
The pressure dims and weight becomes light,
I feel more safe, I feel more right.

Maybe I'm speaking, perhaps you hear,
the many ways past what sounds appear.
My hands in yours, help me feel strong,
in your eyes, I now feel I belong.

I'm learning to grow and to be okay,

even if my words aren't coming today.

The dreams we have, do not look the same,

but they're mine to build, without any shame.

Published by Tash Talks Communication
www.tashhowlett.com

family
brightness
sun
trust
comfort
home
peace
joy
forever
mum
soul

www.ingramcontent.com/pod-product-compliance
Lightning Source LLC
Chambersburg PA
CBHW041507220426
43661CB00017B/1269